ALBÉNIZ

MW01011816

CANTOS DE ESPAÑA OPUS 232
FOR THE PIANO

EDITED BY OLGA LLANO KUEHL-WHITE

AN ALFRED MASTERWORK EDITION

Alfred

Copyright © 2017 by Alfred Music
All rights reserved.   Printed in USA.
ISBN-10: 1-4706-3955-6
ISBN-13: 978-1-4706-3955-6

Cover art: El Jaleo *(1882)*
by John Singer Sargent (American, 1856–1925)
Oil on canvas

ISAAC ALBÉNIZ

Contents

Cantos de España, Op. 232
Edited by Olga Llano Kuehl-White

ABOUT THE COMPOSER

Foreword

The music of Spanish composer Isaac Albéniz mirrors his life—both are colorful and passionate. For over 100 years, biographical information on Albéniz has included several falsehoods, including stories that he stowed away on ships and that he studied with Franz Liszt. Albéniz himself often gave exaggerations to embellish his career, even though in reality he led a very charmed life. As a brilliant pianist, he toured successfully and extensively in his country and abroad. In the last two decades of his life, his interest turned more intensively to the composition of opera, *zarzuela* (a Spanish lyric-dramatic genre that alternates between spoken and sung scenes), vocal music, and music for piano. As one of Spain's most outstanding musicians, his works for piano—especially those in a Spanish idiom—are indisputably his lasting legacy.

Isaac Manuel Francisco Albéniz y Pascual was born in Camprodon, a province of Girona in Catalonia, Spain, on May 29, 1860. A child prodigy, he was introduced to the piano by his talented sister, Clementina. At age 8, he entered the Real Conservatorio in Madrid, and by age 12, he was performing throughout Spain. When his father, a customs official, temporarily accepted a government position in Cuba, Albéniz gave performances in Havana and Puerto Rico.

After returning to Spain, Albéniz and his mother traveled to Germany, where he studied briefly at the Leipzig Hochschule für Musik, followed by three years at the Conservatoire royal in Brussels (the latter financed by Count Guillermo Morphy, secretary to King Alfonso XII). Albéniz soon began playing concerts frequently and with great success. In 1880, he traveled to Vienna, Prague, and Budapest, where he had hoped to study with the great pianist Franz Liszt (1811–1886), only to find him away on tour. Not wanting to disappoint his father, who had subsidized the trip, Albéniz concocted a story about studying with the legendary musician.

At the age of 23, Albéniz moved to Barcelona, where he eventually married one of his students, Rosina Jordana Lagarriga (1863–1945). Around the same time, he met Felipe Pedrell (1841–1922), a teacher, musicologist, and opera composer. Pedrell was a strong advocate of Spanish nationalism and provided the creative impetus that Albéniz needed, encouraging him and other composers to utilize the musical elements of Spain's folk songs and dances. Albéniz was especially drawn to *flamenco*, the exotic music of Andalucía, and this was his inspiration for many of his finest works for piano.

At the 1888 Exposición Universal in Barcelona, representatives of the Erard piano manufacturing company heard Albéniz perform and invited him to give a concert in Paris the following year. The concert was attended by composers Gabriel Fauré (1845–1924), Claude Debussy (1862–1918), Maurice Ravel (1875–1937), and Paul Dukas (1865–1935). That same year, Albéniz performed several concerts in London and received critical acclaim.

Although an ardent Spaniard proud of his heritage, Albéniz recognized that the Spanish political and cultural environment was not as conducive for musicians as Paris or London. So, in 1890, he purchased a home in Brompton, England, for his wife and three children. Albéniz toured extensively until the age of 30. He then turned more towards composition during the last two decades of his life. In 1893, Albeniz's manager, Henry Lowenfeld, introduced him to Francis Money-Coutts (1852–1923), who was a poet, librettist, and wealthy heir of the Coutts banking family. Money-Coutts supported Albéniz in return for the composer setting his poetry and librettos to music. Their best collaboration was the opera *Pepita Jiménez*, which was based on a novel by Juan Valera (1824–1905). It was performed in Italian, which was the custom of the time, and premiered in Barcelona in 1896. Many years later, it was translated into Spanish and revised as an opera in three acts by composer Pablo Sorozábal (1897–1988), premiering in Madrid's Teatro de la Zarzuela in 1964.

During his years in England, Albéniz continued to perform throughout Europe both as a soloist and with various orchestras. He also performed a great deal of chamber music in Barcelona. However, many musicians urged him to return to France. Albéniz's wife also preferred Paris since she was more fluent in French than in English. The family moved to Paris in 1894, and their home became a gathering place for writers, musicians, and artists. While in Paris, Albéniz taught piano at the Schola Cantorum, where he also studied counterpoint with Vincent d'Indy (1851–1931) and met French composers Erik Satie (1866–1925), Albert Roussel (1869–1937), and Déodat de Séverac (1872–1921). He had the opportunity to attend premiers of Debussy's works and developed close friendships with both Fauré and Dukas.

In 1905, Albéniz began work on his immortal masterpiece *Iberia*, a collection of 12 pieces for piano evoking Spanish scenes and places. With French influences and a new, enriched harmonic vocabulary, *Iberia* brought Spanish music into the 20th century.

During this same period, Albéniz suffered serious ailments, and his failing kidneys were of grave concern. By 1908, Albéniz's rapidly declining health caused the family to leave Paris in search of cures or restoratives. They went to the islands in the Mediterranean. Many friends visited regularly, including Spanish composer Enrique Granados (1867–1916), who presented him with a letter from Debussy informing Albéniz that he had been awarded the Grand-Croix de la Légion d'honneur, one of France's highest honors. Finally succumbing to Bright's disease, Albéniz died May 18, 1909, in Cambo-les-Bains in the French Pyrenees. Sent by train to Barcelona, he was buried in Cementiri del Sud-oest on the seaward side of historic Montjuïc, a hill overlooking that famous city.

Albéniz created a new musical language for his piano compositions derived from Spain's heritage, which was the inspiration for most of his finest piano works. He was especially drawn to the exotic music of Andalucía, with its multi-cultural heritage. Albéniz often provided the names of Spanish towns and regions for his compositions' titles. As a musical storyteller, Albéniz created tonal portraits depicting geographic areas of his beloved Spain, idiographic of Spanish life by evoking scenes, places, and historical events. Albéniz composed more than 250 works, although many are lost or incomplete. His many collections—which include *España*, Op. 165; *Cantos de España*, Op. 232; *Suite Española No. 1*, Op. 47; *Recuerdos de Viaje*, Op. 71; *La Vega*; and his masterwork *Iberia*—exerted discernible influences on succeeding composers worldwide.

ABOUT THIS EDITION

Facsimiles of the first Spanish printing of *Chantes d'Espagne* served as the text for this edition. Past editions follow the imperfect first printing, which was replete with engravers' errors and lacking the interpretive details integral for the artistic performance of Spanish music. In preparing this edition, the editor conducted research in the Real Conservatorio de la Música and the Biblioteca Nacional (both located in Madrid), the Museu de la Música in Barcelona, and the Musical Archives of the British Library in London. The editor studied, performed, and researched the repertoire with renowned pianist and Spanish-music interpreter Alicia de Larrocha (1923–2009) at the Academia Marshall in Barcelona and privately over a period of 30 years, gaining insights into the legacy of performance-practice traditions of Spanish music.

None of the pieces of *Cantos de España* are available in an autograph manuscript. The first three pieces of the collection were published by Juan Bautista Pujol and Co. in Barcelona in 1892, followed by the fourth and fifth pieces in 1897. The "Prélude" and "Seguidillas" composed in the 1880s can also be found in Albéniz's *Suite Española No. 1*, Op. 47. The major differences between the versions found in the *Suite Española* and the versions in *Cantos de España* consist of rhythmic and dynamic changes.

EDITORIAL AND PERFORMANCE CONSIDERATIONS

The editor has sought to fix errors found in previous editions by correcting musical inaccuracies and providing clarification on appropriate stylistic performance and interpretation of Spanish music. Fingerings are editorial, except for those by the composer set in this edition in italics. Phrase and pedaling marks are editorial unless indicated otherwise in footnotes. Regarding fingering and pedaling, one size cannot fit all. Editorial suggestions for pedaling cannot be conclusive since pedaling must be adapted by the performer to adjust to external factors such as the size of the music room or concert hall and the resonance of the instrument.

Articulations and dynamics have been added by the editor in places where such markings can be found in similar passages elsewhere in the music. Additional editorial changes include the correction of notational and rhythmic inaccuracies, as well as the redistribution of notes between the hands for technical and musical fluency. To avoid excessive annotations, in all of these edited passages neither editorial parentheses nor accompanying footnotes have been added. All metronome marks are editorial.

Although not captured in music notation, several artistic refinements are integral to the performance of Spanish music:

- subtly modifying the tempo, to contrast the interchange between lyrical phrases and instrumental phrases;

- applying agogic accents and/or lengthening the value of notes, to allow for expressive freedom;

- employing rubato;

- and artistically using the pedals.

These performance practices and their specific application to *Cantos de España* are further explored in the following "About the Music" section. The editor's main objective is to enlighten pianists in achieving an authentic and artistic interpretation, through a carefully researched edition based on a lifetime of study with the musical guidance of Alicia de Larrocha, thereby preserving the performance practice tradition of Spanish music for future pianists and fulfilling the promise this editor made to her teacher.

ABOUT THE MUSIC

Spain is a land of enchantment, of dreamers and doers; a land of Cervantes and his brave Don Quixote; a land of great painters and great warriors; a land where music sprang from the soil and the soul, providing composers with genuine artistic inspiration. At the heart of Spain's music are songs and dances. Historians have claimed that Spain has more national dances than any other country, due to the influences of many civilizations that inhabited the country.

Elements of Spanish Music

Over centuries, folk elements of past cultures—particularly Arab, Hebraic, and Gypsy—fused together creating the Spanish idiom. With guitar, castanets, hand clapping, and finger snapping, the Gypsies developed the *cante hondo* style, which eventually became the popular *cante flamenco* of today. Representing a musical journey through a variety of emotions, the Spanish idiom conveys both high spirits and a passionate soul, one that will suddenly burst into expressions of great joy or deep sorrow. Harmonically and melodically, its intrinsically exotic atmosphere is derived from Arab-Gypsy modalities, which often resemble Phrygian mode but with a raised 3rd.

Exotic, folk-derived mode

augmented 2nd

Note the distinctive augmented-2nd interval. Other modal inflections are found throughout Spanish music. This characteristic modality results in colorful melodic and harmonic passages and a mysterious ambience that feeds the imagination.

Interpreting Spanish Music

Spanish music, which is often emotionally charged, requires the same artistic refinements as other music and an adherence to the music's stylistic elements in conveying the music's character and interpretation. The *cante hondo*, which is represented in the *copla* (slow, song-like sections), must be played with the proper stylistic sincerity, musical sensitivity, and rhythmic flexibility of an appropriate rubato. However, the essence of Spanish music lies in the strong rhythmic pulse found in its folk dances. This *ritmo de danza* precision cannot be emphasized enough. Its execution should evoke the rhythmic precision of castanets and the elaborate footwork of Spanish dancers. Of particular note, within the triplet figuration common in the castanet idiom, there should be no rubato.

Inspiration for *Cantos de España*

Albéniz found creative inspiration from the legends of Spain's historic past. The beautiful northwestern region of Asturias, where fertile landscapes and snow-capped mountains descend to the Cantabrian Sea, is rich in folklore and folk pride. Surrounded by mountain ranges, the people from Asturias (descendants of the Celts, called the Astures) have been characterized as possessing a persistent and an indomitable spirit. Their special Asturcón ponies were known for their pace and prance and an extraordinary ability in scaling crags and mountains. The rugged terrain proved impenetrable for a mixed Arab-Berber army of Muslim Moors who first attempted an invasion in 714. Headed by a Visigothic nobleman named Pelayo (ca. 685–737), Cantabrians joined forces with the men from the Kingdom of Asturias, and although vastly outnumbered, they defeated the Moors in 722. A statue of the brave Pelayo, who became an Asturian king, stands near the battle site in the national park of Covadonga, gazing defiantly towards the surrounding mountains.

While a persistent alternating-hands theme commands the tumultuous **A** sections of this *Prélude*, Albéniz utilizes a spirited equestrian rhythm, mounting in excitement, which musically evokes the historic battle of the Asturians and the Moors. The expressive **B** section, or *copla*, begins with a melodic declamation of *cante hondo* in measures 63–65, answered by two chords in measures 65–66. According to de Larrocha, in the Spanish performance-practice tradition these chords would be performed by a guitar, played arpeggiated as in the strumming *rasgueado* technique.

"Prélude" (excerpt), mm. 63–66, with cante hondo *style and* rasgueado *strums*

Integral to the Spanish idiom are frequent changes in tempo, requiring artistic handling of rubato for expressive freedom. A dance-like theme is introduced in measure 88 and expanded with increased animation in measures 100–106. De Larrocha recommended the redistribution of notes in measures 100–103 and in similar passages throughout this work. The frequent use of upper mordents suggests castanets, which traditionally accompany singers and dancers, adding flashes of color to the musical tapestry. Measures 112–114 signal the brief presence of the ominous equestrian theme, foretelling the reprise of the brilliant **A** section in measure 123.

Orientale uses those characteristic elements of the Spanish idiom that include clear tonal centers utilizing the exotic Hispano-Arab modal patterns, dance-like rhythms, and expressive melodies that exhibit the chromatic inflection integral to the Andalucían folk cultures. The brief four-measure introduction, with its exotic Middle Eastern overtones, sets the scene and the mood for the spirited dance. Beginning at measure 5, the popular rhythmic triplets of castanets join the arpeggiated bass chords typical of the guitar's *rasgueado* technique. Measures 24–30 display the musical elements of the heel-stamping solo dance called *zapateado*, in which rhythmic vigor is allied with vivid color. The bass pedal point, on the pitch A, and the well-articulated staccato passages suggest an exotic modality. This can be seen, for example, in the tetrachord A–B-flat–C-sharp–D in measures 10, 24, and 28.

"Orientale" (excerpt), m. 10, displaying exotic modality

A second theme appearing in measure 33 in F major is combined in measure 41 with an expressive soprano melody, designated *cantando* (singing). The music unfolds reaching levels of *ff*, and there is a display in measures 60–63 of cascading chromatic notes. A reprise of the first theme occurs in measures 64–89 before a harmonic modulation to D major for the second theme at measure 90. Measures 105, 109, and 111 feature colorful augmented 2nds and lead into the *zapateado* of measures 117–124. Gradually, the music fades away to a *ppp* before a final resounding *fff*.

Spain's array of national dances stem from the influences of the many civilizations that inhabited Spain. Subtitled "Danse Espagnole," *Sous le palmier* (*Under the Palm Tree*) conveys characteristics of a *habanera*, the Cuban dance of Spanish origin. Observe the inner melodic line of the four-measure introduction marked *marcato*. At measure 5, the bass provides a swaying rhythm that creates a pleasant ambience for the music's sentimentality, which is both tender and nostalgic. The expressive melody beginning at measure 5 requires voicing, legato fingering, and a delayed or legato pedaling.

"Sous le palmier" (excerpt), mm. 5–7,
with habanera *rhythms and an expressive melody*

Integral to the dance are frequent fluctuations of tempo, seen in measures 10, 12, 13, 24, 25, and similar measures. The modulation at measure 35 to B-flat major continues the rhythm of the dance, with the upper mordents and triplets suggesting castanet embellishments.

Albéniz found inspiration in the folk music of Andalucía, which would not exist without the guitar. It traditionally accompanied the songs and dances, and it is rhythmically suggested in this piece, in the treble chords which can be arpeggiated. The music returns briefly to the **A** section in measures 59–70. Although this piece is not particularly difficult technically, the final page requires emotional expression coupled with musical artistry to convey the subtleties of rubato and tempo changes as well as the whispering softness of *pp* and *ppp*. In measure 73, the first note in the treble should receive an agogic inflection and be held longer for its expressive intent. There is a charming sequential digression in measures 81–88, a return of the dance in measures 89–96, and finally a gradual fading away in measures 97–100 that imparts the tenderness of a reluctant farewell.

Don Pelayo, rey de Asturias (ca. 1853–1856)
by Luis de Madrazo (Spanish, 1825–1897)

The city of Córdoba, which is in the region of Andalucía, was the capital of Spain during the occupation of the Moors. It is one of Spain's most interesting and historically important cities, with a famous cathedral, the magnificent Mezquita (or Great Mosque), and the 14th-century Jewish Synagogue serving as a visual reminder of Spain's heritage. Like many of Albéniz's pieces, this hauntingly beautiful work was composed as a tonal portrait capturing part of Spain's history.

On large canvases, the great Spanish painters Francisco Goya (1746–1828) and Pablo Picasso (1881–1973) portrayed the ravages of war. In *Córdoba*, Albéniz depicts a war-torn scene, substantiating music's ability to resonate above the brutality of war. This unusual composition is a veritable Spanish treasure that magically depicts the fiery spirit and passion of Spanish music.

Albéniz set the prevailing mood for this piece by prefacing the music with the following epigraph (translated by the editor):

> *In the silence of the night, interrupted by whispering jasmine-scented breezes, are heard the guzlas accompanying the Serenades and spreading into the air ardent melodies and notes as sweet as the swaying palm trees in the celestial heavens.*

The work begins with a bass pedal point in measures 1–20 found below a chant-like soprano melody moving within chordal progressions. This creates a serious atmosphere that recalls music sung by Spanish monks during religious processions. Measure 38 announces the first theme, which retains the somber ambience. At measure 53, there is a tempo change (*Allegro*) and rhythmic transformation to the familiar sounds of a festive celebration. This section portrays singers as well as castanet-playing dancers, as seen in the upper mordents of measure 59, 61, and 67. The second theme, first presented in measure 57, requires skillful melodic voicing. De Larrocha provided fingerings and the redistribution of notes for technical and musical facility in measure 78 and in all the ensuing measures where there is an exchange between the hands. Loud rumblings heard in the bass tremolos of measures 133–141 suddenly interrupt the exuberant spirit, and in measures 137–140 a compellingly sad bugle (which de Larrocha referred to as a "trompetilla") persuasively conveys an embattled scene.

"Córdoba" (excerpt), mm. 137–140,
with a right-hand bugle call

There is another somber religious procession at measure 149 followed by a less festive celebration at measure 156 with a return of the dance.

The title of this piece, *Seguidillas*, is the name of a popular Spanish dance in triple meter, in which repeated guitar figures suggesting dance passages alternate with song phrases. This composition is one of Albéniz's most famous works. In an extended ternary form, the piece begins with a primary theme of dance rhythms in measures 1–14, conveying the idiomatic sounds of the castanets that traditionally accompany Spanish dancers. The song-like secondary theme of measures 15–17, 28–30, and 41–43 is interspersed between the dance-like passages of measures 18–27, 31–40, and 44–53. Editorial suggestions are given in these passages for the redistribution of notes between the hands for technical and musical facility. A *copla* comprises measures 54–69. There is an emotional exchange between measures 54–56 and the spirited outbursts of harmonic color in the dance-like "castanet" response of measure 57. Measures 58–61 appear in the exotic Arab-Andalucían mode of A–B-flat–C-sharp–D–E–F–G–A.

"Seguidillas" (excerpt), mm. 58–61, displaying Arab-Andalucían mode

Measures 70–101 are an extended development of the thematic material, treated sequentially and enveloped in a contrapuntal texture that allows for interesting harmonic progressions. Measure 102 confirms a return to the original tonal center of F-sharp major, with a transformed secondary theme boldly displayed. An exuberant intensity prevails, which continues to build in excitement for a brilliant finale.

Isaac Albéniz y Pascual (1894)
by Ramón Casas (Spanish, 1866–1932)

GLOSSARY OF SPANISH TERMS

Andalucía – the southern region of Spain comprising the cities of Almería, Cádiz, Córdoba, Granada, Huelva, Jaén, Málaga, and Sevilla. The region is known for its *cante flamenco*.

cante flamenco – a song style developed from early 19th-century *cante hondo* with Middle Eastern influences. By the late 19th century, gypsies adopted the *cante hondo*, renaming it *cante flamenco*.

cante hondo (cante jondo) – of Byzantine and Jewish origin, *cante hondo* is a melancholy song with repetition of short phrases, an absence of strict meter, expressive ornamentation, and a tragic mood. It is often found in the middle section of ternary forms or presented intermittently around dance-like passages.

copla – a stanza or refrain of the *cante hondo*. The Andalucían *copla* is intensely passionate.

cuadro flamenco – an ensemble that includes dancers, singers, and guitarists sitting in a semi-circle.

flamenco – stylistic performances of folk songs and dances accompanied by guitar and castanets, particularly represented in southern Spain's Andalucían region.

jaleos – loud hand clapping and shouted words of encouragement from spectators during an Andalucían dance.

jota – originating from the region of Aragon, a *jota* is a dance in moderate to rapid triple time. Traditionally, it expressed the theme of courtship.

La Alhambra – the palace in Granada built by the Moors, the mixed Arab and Berber conquerors of Spain.

palmadas – rhythmic hand clapping of dancers.

pitos – finger snaps accompanying gypsy dancers, traditionally favored over the castanets by artistic purists.

punteado – a common guitar technique of plucking the strings with the right-hand fingertips, to play individual notes in succession. *Punteado* may also refer to the acoustic effect of rapid finger strokes on the wooden rim of the guitar.

rasgueado – a common guitar technique of strumming the strings to produce chordal effects and arpeggios.

seguidillas – a highly popular dance in which repeated guitar passages suggesting dance-like phrases alternate with lyrical phrases in a quick triple meter.

taconeos – Spanish dancers' stamping heels, displayed during the Spanish dance called the *zapateado*.

zapateado – a fast Spanish dance in which the dancers engage in rapid stamping of the heels (from the Spanish word *zapata*, meaning shoe).

Cantos de España

À mon cher ami Louis E. Pujol

Prélude

Isaac Albéniz (1860–1909)
Op. 232

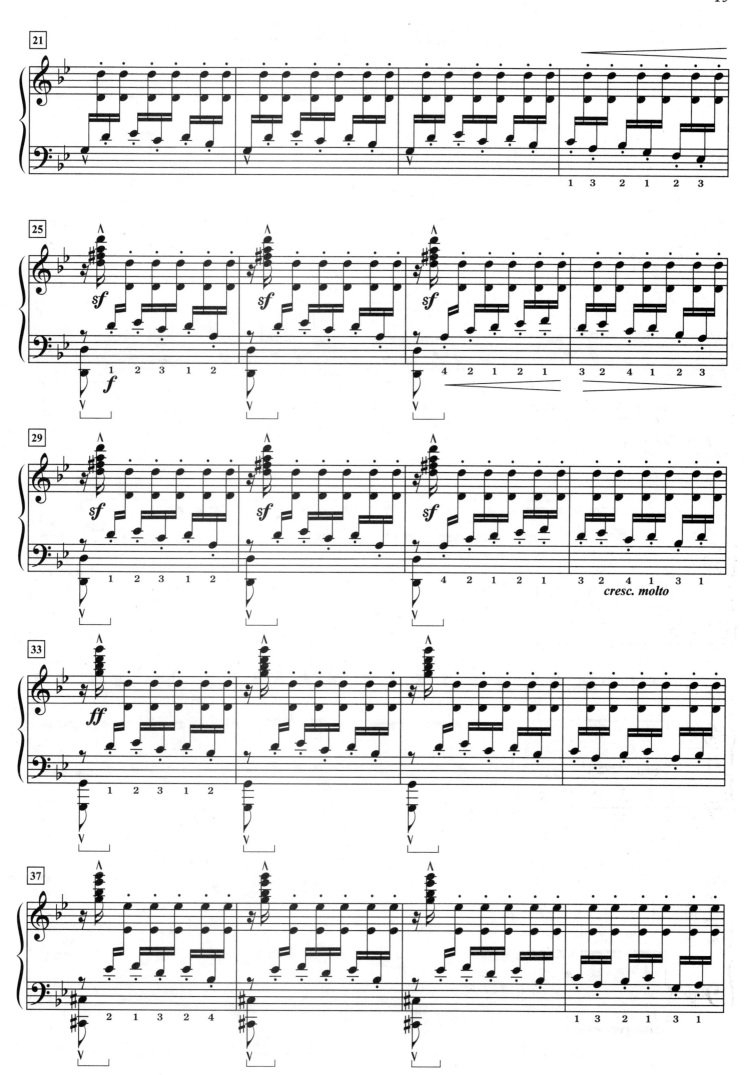

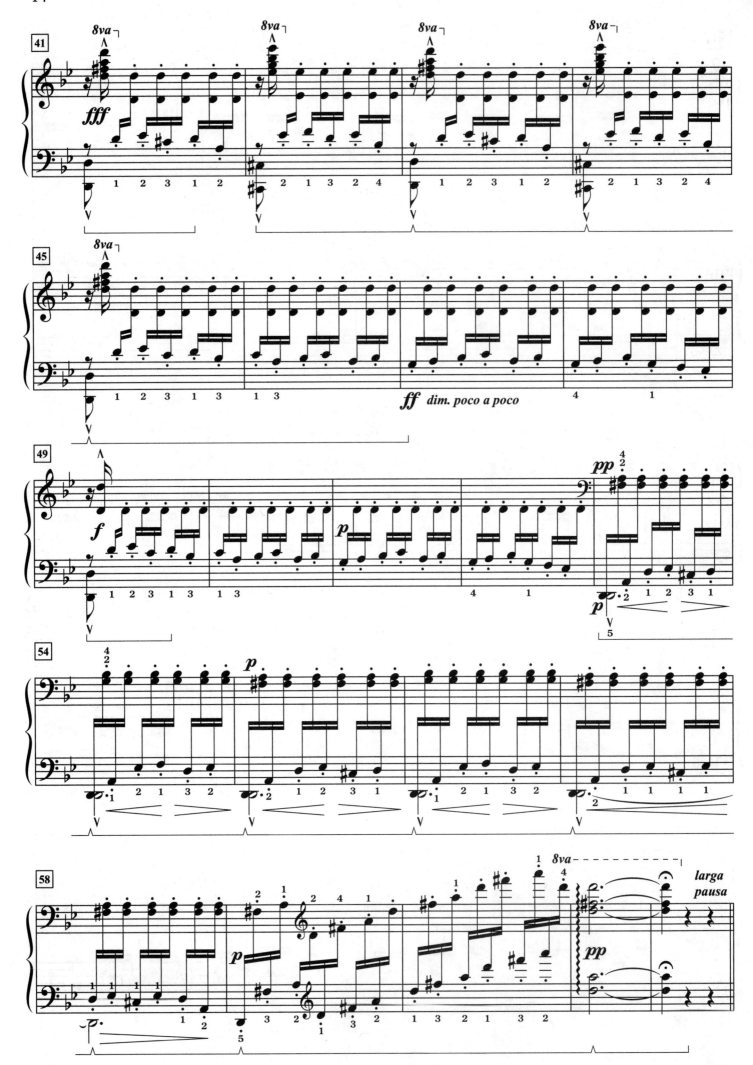

(a) Upper mordent on the beat:

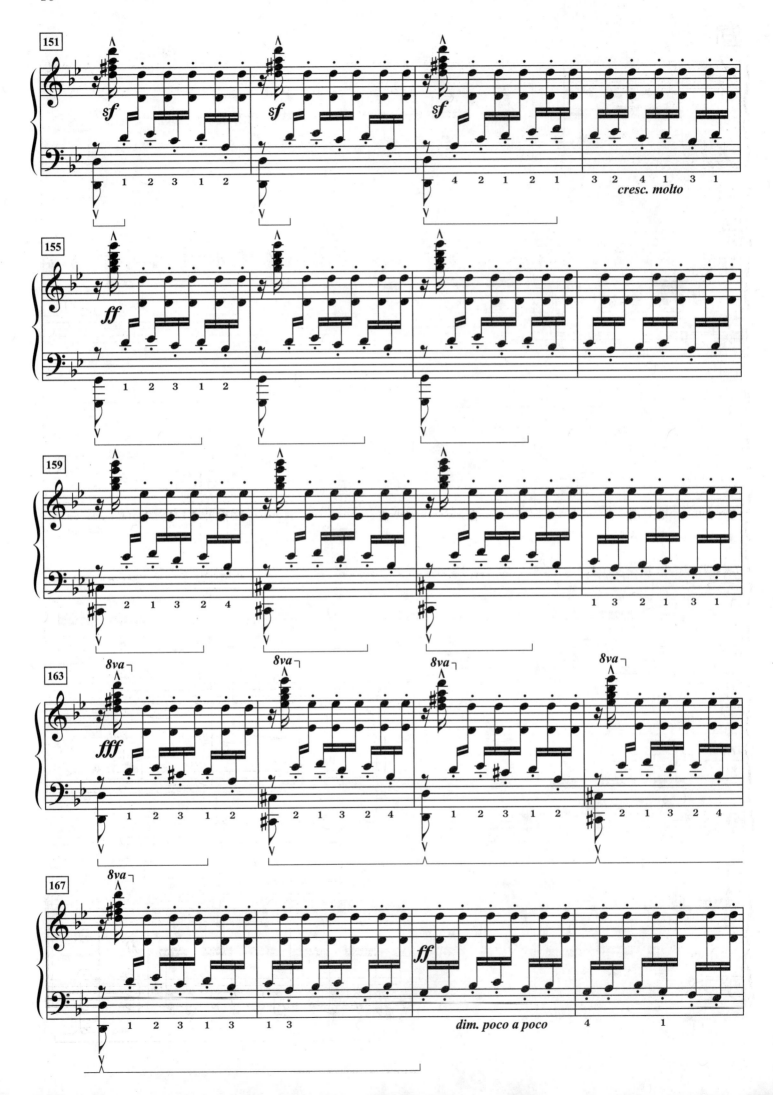

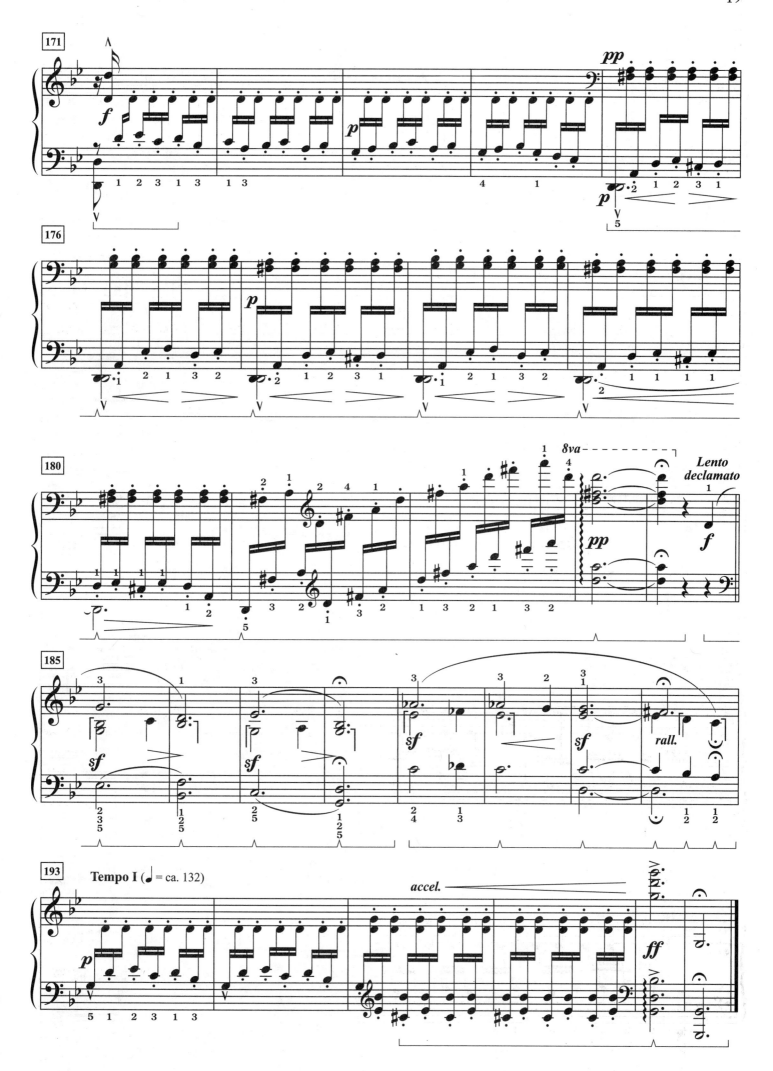

À mon ami et ancien élève Joaquin Bonnin

Orientale

(a) On the beat.

À Emilio Vilalta

Sous le palmier
(Danse Espagnole)

À Enrique Morera

Córdoba

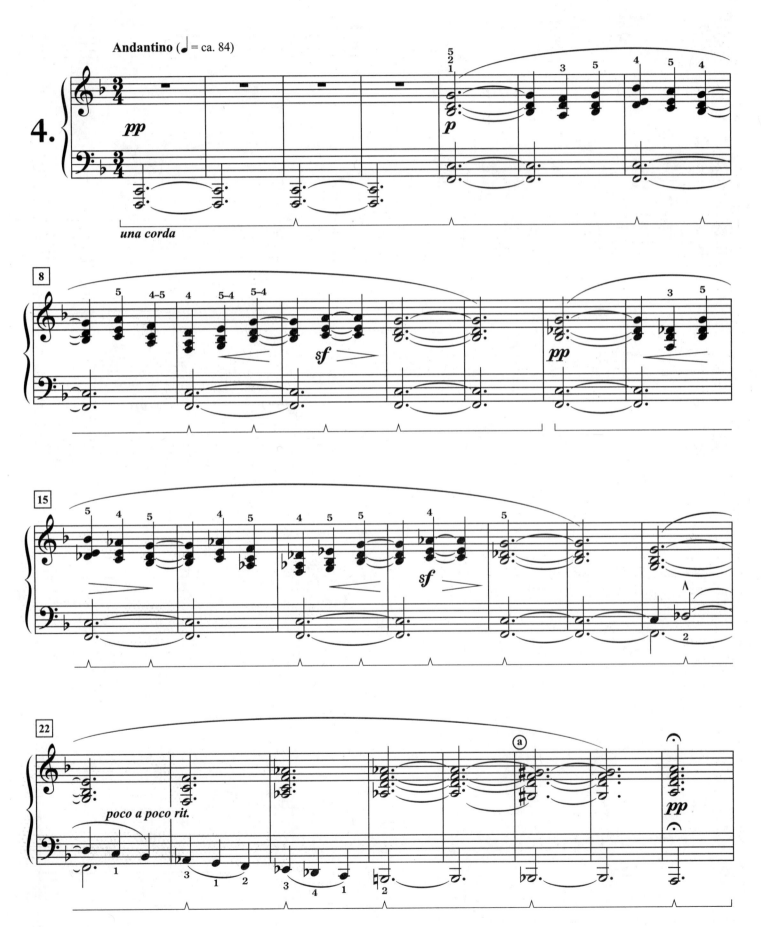

ⓐ The chord is tied.

ⓒ Bring out the bugle call.

36

(d) Gradually release the pedal.

(e) Gradually release the pedal.

À Leonardo Moyua (Leo de Silka)

Seguidillas

(a) Left hand turned sideways above the right hand.

ⓓ Small hands may omit the lowest note.